RISE

RISE

A Collection of Inspirational Poetry,
Prose, and Affirmations.

Shana Danielle

The Shana Danielle Company, LLC
Camden, NJ

RISE

This is a work of non-fiction. All poems in this book are original works of the author. Any similarities to other works are coincidental. This publication is designed to educate and provide general information regarding the subject matter based on the author's experiences. It is published with the understanding that neither the author nor the publisher is engaged in rendering professional counseling services. Each situation is different, and the advice should be tailored to particular circumstances.

Any internet addresses, phone numbers, or company or product information printed in this book are offered as a resource and are not intended in any way to be or to imply an endorsement by The Shana Danielle Company, nor does The Shana Danielle Company vouch for the existence, content, or services of these sites, phone numbers, companies, or products beyond the life of this book.

RISE © 2020 Shana Davis

All rights reserved. No part of this publication may be recorded, stored in a retrieval system, or transmitted in any form or by any means, electronic, mechanical, photocopied, recorded or otherwise, without prior written permission from the publisher.

ISBN-13: 978-1-7353806-0-5

Published by The Shana Danielle Company LLC
Camden, NJ

Printed in the United States of America
First Edition August 2020

Cover Design: Michael Corvin
Interior Design: Make Your Mark Publishing Solutions
Editing: Make Your Mark Publishing Solutions

Version. Rights in the Authorized Version in the United Kingdom are vested in the Crown. Reproduced by permission of the Crown's patentee, Cambridge University Press.

Scripture taken from the New King James Version. Copyright © 1982 by Thomas Nelson, Inc. Used by permission. All rights reserved.

Scripture quotations marked (NLT) are taken from the Holy Bible, New Living Translation, copyright ©1996, 2004, 2015 by Tyndale House Foundation. Used by permission of Tyndale House Publishers, a Division of Tyndale House Ministries, Carol Stream, Illinois 60188. All rights reserved.

Scripture quotations marked MSG are taken from THE MESSAGE, copyright © 1993, 2002, 2018 by Eugene H. Peterson. Used by permission of NavPress. All rights reserved. Represented by Tyndale House Publishers, a Division of Tyndale House Ministries.

Scripture quotations marked (NIV) are taken from the Holy Bible, New International Version®, NIV®. Copyright © 1973, 1978, 1984, 2011 by Biblica, Inc.™ Used by permission of Zondervan. All rights reserved worldwide. www.zondervan.com The "NIV" and "New International Version" are trademarks registered in the United States Patent and Trademark Office by Biblica, Inc.™

All Scripture quotations are from The Passion Translation®. Copyright © 2017, 2018 by Passion & Fire Ministries, Inc. Used by permission. All rights reserved. ThePassionTranslation.com.

In Loving Memory of Leon William Davis.
Without you pushing me to let my light shine,
the young woman who wrote this book
would have remained timid, locked in her shell,
and **Rise** *would have never come to fruition.*
Thank you.
I love you forever, Daddy.
Happy Birthday.
10/24/1941 – 03/30/2017

This book is dedicated to everyone dealing with different struggles in life–anyone who has ever felt lost, hurt, anxious, stressed, unaccepted, but desires healing. You are not alone.

It is my prayer that the words on these pages will impact your soul and motivate you to rise above any obstacle preventing you from achieving your purpose.

I pray you find peace as you begin your journey, discovering genuine self-love and the unashamed version of you. I pray that this book inspires, motivates, and rejuvenates your life in a tremendous way.

As you read, I challenge you to reflect on your own emotional wounds and seek healing, continually looking for ways to improve yourself and rise.

Contents

Dedication vi

PART ONE | FREE YOURSELF
Introduction 4
One | **Black Poet** 9
Two | **Barbie** 15
Three | **Black Is Beautiful** 25
Four | **On the Rise** 35

PART TWO | I CAN. I WILL. I MUST
Focus 45
Five | **Four Hundred Years** 49
Six | **Success** 63
Seven | **Time** 77
Eight | **Shoes** 85

PART THREE | LET IT GO
Be Vulnerable 97
Nine | **Black and Blue** 101
Ten | **The Fall** 115
Eleven | **Rise** 127
Twelve | **Voices** 133

Acknowledgments 143

PART ONE

Rise

Free Yourself.

> "If there is a book that
> you want to read,
> but it hasn't been written yet,
> you must be the one to write it."
> —Toni Morrison

Seven years. For seven years, I had the idea to write this book, but never started the process—not because I struggled with what to write, but because I feared the opinions of other people. I obsessed over what bad things people would say, and I allowed those fears to steal seven years.

During that time, I went through some of the worst storms of my life, and I sought help from many different people in many different places—mostly the wrong people in the wrong places, who helped feed my fears. In the most tumultuous storm of my life, I shared my biggest fears with the wrong person, when I should have taken all those fears to God. The enemy worked through this individual, an individual who, without suggestions from the enemy, is an amazing, beautiful, delightful blessing to be around. The enemy, who comes to kill, steal, and destroy anything good, worked through this person as a vessel and began to attack me like I've never been attacked before.

The attacks from the enemy caused me to almost give up on everything. I almost gave up my marriage, my dreams, my faith, and my high self-esteem. The little glimmer of light I had was almost snuffed out. But the Holy Spirit told me to take one more chance, one more leap of faith, and I shared with one more person the fears and added anxiety placed in me by the enemy during this storm. Y'all, God worked through this mighty, magnificent, virtuous person. God's love radiated so much in this person's life that when it shined on me, I felt as if I could be Peter walking on the Sea of Galilee.

I then got back into my Word and began to pray like never before. God spoke to me, and I listened more—listened to who He called me to be. I meditated on the truth that I was made in His image (Genesis 2:7), I am fearfully and wonderfully made (Psalms 139:14), and He came so

I may have life and have life more abundantly (John 10:10). I started chasing after God and began to obsess over what He said about me.

A miraculous shift happened. I came to have a newfound love for myself and for others. I became a better parent and a better wife. I became a better child of God and a better reflection of His love. My relationship with the Father became so much better as I believed who He called me to be and the gifts He had in store for me.

Stronger than ever, I confidently would bind the lies that the enemy said about me—lies about not being good enough, not being pretty enough, and not having the strength to endure difficult seasons in my life. The more I exercised my faith, cast down those lies, and believed God's truths, the less impact the lies had on me.

When fears and insecurities now start to come my way, they bounce off and no longer stay with me. I am now courageous enough to share my writings with the world. This book is meant to encourage everyone, regardless of your background, struggles or wounds, to push through, survive, love yourself, and rise.

I Forgive You

Not because you apologized
Or owned your web of lies,
But because I realize
It will help the pain subside.

My soul identified
Needing healing, not demise.
No more tears in my eyes.
"Restoration!" Spirit cried.

Forgiveness. I survived.
Dancing, I feel alive.
Peace no longer hides.
Forgiveness now resides.

Shana Danielle

THEIR PERCEPTION DOES NOT MATTER. I KNOW WHO I AM!

— Shana Danielle

"God didn't set us up for an angry rejection but for salvation by our Master, Jesus Christ. He died for us, a death that triggered life. Whether we're awake with the living or asleep with the dead, we're alive with him! So speak encouraging words to one another. Build up hope so you'll all be together in this, no one left out, no one left behind. I know you're already doing this; just keep on doing it."
1 Thessalonians 5:9-11 MSG

Throughout this book, you will see Bible verses towards the end of each chapter. Different translations that may be easier to read are provided.

ONE

"Never be limited by other people's limited imaginations."

—Dr. Mae Jemison

Shana Danielle

BLACK POET

Beautiful   **P**ositive

Loving   **O**riginal

Awesome   **E**xtraordinary

Creative   **T**eacher

Knowledgeable

Sometimes it rhymes and sometimes it does not,
But there is a message, whether you like it or not.
I'm sorry, Beach Boy, that you can't ride the wave of my words,
But my poetry is inspirational, and it needs to be heard.

Do not compare me to the likes of Lil' Kim.
I am a Queen both out and in,
But no, I am not a "Queen B";
I am a Queen uplifting people's mentality.

I write for people to grow, not to keep them down.
You are an uninvited critic—you're a joke; you're a clown.
You try to discourage me and make me frown.
That's why you get no attention. I don't need that around.

Rise

I'm sorry, Mr. Rock Star, if you think my lyrics are not up to par;
But if I write on your level, I will never go far.
I do not need your approval to drive this car
For He has chosen me to reach the stars.

I'm sorry, Mr. Country Roller,
that my lines don't jive to the tune of your controller.
You think I couldn't have anything significant to say
Because I am young and black—but I am proud today.

Do not compare me to Nicki Minaj or Cardi B;
You will respect my individuality.
I guess because I am young and I'm black,
Everything I say must be someone else's rap.

And yes, all rap is—is poetry to music,
But for you to comprehend it would be like solving a Rubik's.
Maybe if I were Edgar Allan Poe,
You could understand my poetic flow.

But I can only be me, a female black poet.
I've been given a light, not to hide but to show it.
I am a wonderful, talented poet,
And I don't need acceptance from anyone else to know it.

While I was employed as a correctional officer earlier in my life, I shared with some people my dream of becoming an entrepreneur, author, and inspirational speaker. Some people were heavily in my corner, excitedly saying, "Go, girl! You can do this," "I'm so happy for you and can't wait to buy your book," and "Your poetry is going to change the world."

On the other hand, there were some other select individuals who were less than enthusiastic and would put me down. They would laugh and say things like: "You're never going to become an author"; "What are you, rapping? Who do you think you are? Little Kim?"; and "There's nothing for you outside of this building. You'll always work here; there is nothing better. If you leave here, you'll just be a greeter at Walmart. There isn't a better life outside of this jail."

It was in those moments that I learned not to share my dreams or vision with everyone. I felt discouraged and needed to encourage myself before I could encourage other people. It took me seven years to build up the courage to even start to put together this book of encouragement. However, once I did, my determination became like that of a pilot trying to land a 747 on the Hudson.

I resolved to write this book of inspiration and push it to as many people as possible. While every topic may not apply to you, my hope is that a piece resonates and encourages you.

My goal:
To inspire you to Rise.

> "The Lord is a refuge for the oppressed, a stronghold in times of trouble. Those who know your name trust in you, for you, Lord, have never forsaken those who seek you."
> **Psalms 9:9-10 NIV**

NEVER LET SOMEONE ELSE'S VIEW DETERMINE HOW YOU SEE YOU.

—Shana Danielle

TWO

Rise

"Change will not come if we wait for some other person or some other time.

We are the ones we've been waiting for.

We are the change that we seek."

—Barack Obama

Shana Danielle

Barbie

Barbie,
Perfectly Plastic.
Barbie,
You look so fantastic.
With yo' midriff, high heels, and short skirts.
Barbie,
How much are you worth?
"Huh?"
You got traded: *paper* for *plastic*.
Barbie,
All that wax–you can have it.
With yo' fake mass, nose, eyes, and breasts,
Got little girls stuffin' training bras
Looking for a toy chest.

                Playboy, Maxim, Penthouse, King
        These are the "Barbies" young girls try to be.
                       We need to change
                         The mentality
                     That our sexuality
                    Is only sensuality–
                    Open up our eyes
                And come to the reality

Rise

That
You are an original, not a copy.
Silicone, plastic, botox bodies
Lypo, injections–
Everybody circumventin'
Being an individual.
Y'all would rather be,
Someone else's invention.

Barbie,
You's a "**Bad** Chick," You's a "**Five-Star** Chick"
*Is it no longer degrading because he added a **prefix**?*
"***Dime*** Chick," "***Fly*** Chick," "***Ride or Die*** Chick"—
Are all those names acceptable … if that joker hood rich?

Now, I was raised knowing I was a Queen.
I didn't know it entailed showin' my tail on a screen.
Society really twisted our point of view—
Made us think to be loved, rich *hittas* we gotta screw.

Shana Danielle

And after they're done,
They move on to the next one,
Looking for a new Barbie—
Guess you malfunctioned.

Oh well … it starts again.
X-rated pictures on Instagram and Twitter
Chicks becoming bitter
Sayin, "Ain't no real men. **_ALL_** _jokers_ is quitters."
Listen to what you said,
"*Jokers*" instead of "*men*"
There's a difference …
<u>Boys</u> only pretend.

Jokers say they love you
But always leave you alone,
Making you the appetizer
While they got their entrée at home.
Yet you showin' off your body,
For a little attention
From a tall boy …
May I make a suggestion?

Realize you AND your body are a temple.
Make sure he comes correct—
Credentials are essential—
And be sure he's fulfilling
His fullest potential.
Potential to be

Rise

Exceptional.
Able to see past
A two-dimensional.

Only a real man can know how to love,
So why sell yourself short and settle for a scrub?
You have the power to turn a boy into a man,
But you have to know your worth
And make your demands.

Every King needs a Queen
Look at the Obamas.
You deserve to be more
Than just some baby mama.

Women were created from a man's rib
We are to stand by his side
Do more than just bear his kids.

Take control of the power you were given.
Pinocchio became a REAL boy.
Barbies,
It's time to become REAL women.

Growing up, it was hard trying to find where I fit into society. I was raised in the church and knew who God called me to be, a virtuous woman. But when I went to school, it seemed the only girls that got attention were the ones who would dress provocatively. My best friend was raised in the Pentecostal church and was only allowed to wear long, flowing skirts. She would come to school and change into pants or shorts just to try to fit in. If we didn't fit in with the other kids, we learned quickly that we would get teased.

As I became an adult, I struggled with some of the "Barbie" philosophies. I contemplated getting a Brazilian butt lift, a surgery to try to keep the "boy" I had. After that situation did not work, I figured if I got the surgery I could attract one that was *ballin'* and I could live a *five-star* life. It was a vicious merry-go-round I was on, trying to fit into culture. The merry-go-round seemed fun at first, but as I kept spinning in circle after circle after circle, I started to get dizzy and not feel so well on the inside.

I learned it is hard to fit into culture because culture is always changing. One day it's perms, the next it's "be natural." One day it's high-waist jeans, the next it's mini skirts. One day it's team dark-skin, the next it's team light-skin. So, I got off the culture train and made a resolve to be who God called me to be. Who did He call you to be?

Rise.

> *"Who can find a virtuous woman? For her price is far above rubies."*
> **Proverbs 31:10 KJV**

Rise

LOVE YOURSELF!

—Shana Danielle

Shana Danielle

BE SMART

You think I want you to give me the world?
Diamonds and purses? Rubies and pearls?
No. My deepest desire is for our worlds to twirl
'Til it looks like a Cream Saver, perfectly swirled.

Longing to be accepted
Protected, not rejected
There's power when we're connected.
Why won't you just accept it?
Stop making me feel neglected …
    "Enough!"
              the Spirit interjected.
Stop looking to be respected
By others; it's demented.
Love, I invented.
    Trust in Me
        and I'll correct it.

Start
Loving on you, a lesson to be taught.
Think on good, pure and sweet and lovely thoughts.
Above all else, you must guard your heart
For out of it flows life.
    Be careful.
        Be smart.

I am Beautiful.
I am Strong.
I am Smart.
I can do
ANYTHING!

—Shana Danielle

THREE

Rise

"I need to see my own beauty and to continue
to be reminded that I am enough,
that I am worthy of love without effort,
that I am beautiful,
that the texture of my hair
and that the shape of my curves,
the size of my lips,
the color of my skin,
and the feelings that I have are all worthy and okay."
—Tracee Ellis Ross

Shana Danielle

BLACK IS BEAUTIFUL

Shhh.
"Keep it to yourself."
Be quiet.
"Never tell 'em how you've felt."
If she admits it,
they become real—
These thoughts she keeps having
and doesn't want to feel.

Her biggest dream
Was to one day be light.
She prayed to God
With all of her might.
Her skin was too dark;
She blended with night.
An over-baked turkey,
She just wasn't cooked right.

Now, don't get it wrong,
She still wanted to be brown,
But a much lighter shade
Would turn it around.
Anything she would have paid
To not look like a field slave,
To be the color of a Band-Aid—
    She'd take these thoughts to her grave.

Rise

She whispered,
>"Lord, give me the magic cream
>To make me the complexion of my dreams;
>Allow me to be part of the light-skinned team,
>Coffee with more than a splash of cream."

It seemed her prayer fell on deaf ears
'Cause every day she woke with silent tears
And then she would hear
From colleagues and peers,
>"You are pretty ...
>>***for a dark-skinned girl.***

Hearing them say that
Made her want to hurl.
They could have just said,
"You're pretty. You're beautiful."
But they had to add a "for a,"
leaving her to feel pitiful.

She was only tolerated
Not accepted by her people
She hoped to be exonerated.
Inclusion that was real,
Not the type that was obligated.
We were all made by God
Why was this so *complicated?*

As people looked her way
They could only see past her.

Shana Danielle

To create their celebrity,
As they walked by, they'd add her—
Add her complexion
to the butt of a joke.
Cruel things, like
she was darker than smoke.

They pretended to love her
In the dark or in secret.
For years she hid in the closet,
Hiding her uniqueness.

Then she prayed,
    "Teach me how to love myself,
    To walk with my head held high,
    Proud of the skin I've been dealt."

She confessed,
    "I.
    Am.
    A.
    Beautiful, Brilliant, Black, Hershey Kiss Dream,
    A Majestic, Exquisite, Resilient, Powerful Queen
    Drizzled in chocolate
    That'll make you scream.

    "Aaaaahhhhh!"

This skin, this capsule for my spirit,
Just doesn't mix or rhyme with this world's lyrics.

Rise

It is deep ... rich,
the color of Mother Earth.
Full of nutrients,
like milk after birth.
Able to thrive like cacti in the desert.
Like the tree giving oxygen, life she exerts.

I am beautiful.
You are beautiful
With that rich
Chocolate color brown.
Black is beautiful.
I like how that sounds.

I'll have a large coffee
with sugar, no cream
And that Ghirardelli Chocolate
Brownie Supreme.

Black is beautiful.
You are beautiful.
I am beautiful.
We are beautiful.

Shana Danielle

LOOK IN THE MIRROR ...

YOU ARE **BEAUTIFUL** QUEEN!

—Shana Danielle

Rise

As a child, I spent years wanting to be light-skinned like my friends and cousins. I spent my early childhood years in the predominately Caucasian town of Runnemede, in the southern part of New Jersey. I lived there until the fifth grade, and then my family transitioned to a more diverse suburb.

I had fun as a child, but while in Runnemede, I never saw reflections of myself anywhere in a position of power. My teachers, friends, and their parents were all of European descent. Most tried to be nice to me, the best they knew how, but they had so many questions about my hair, my nose, my skin and its deep complexion. The one that bothered me most was, "Can I touch your hair?"

Then, there were people in my life who were not so nice. Ironically, my negative interactions did not come only from Caucasians. Many came from black family and friends of a lighter persuasion. Some of the phrases I heard repeatedly as a child were "Blackie," "Gorilla," "Monkey," "Celie," "Color Purple" or, "You crispy, crackly, crunchy, burnt candy bar. You so black you look like tar."

As a child, I did not know how to process those statements. Most adults cannot even process such derogatory expressions; they just become better at finding ways to bury the bad feelings. I learned that submerging my feelings never allowed me to truly deal with them, and they would show up, drowning me in other areas of my life. I went on a journey of learning to love myself and address the insecurities and feelings of inadequacy. It took a lot of strength to face some of my fears and wounded areas. However, I kept God first in the process, and I came to truly love myself.

Rise.

Shana Danielle

> *"Be strong and courageous. Do not be afraid or terrified because of them, for the Lord your God goes with you; he will never leave you nor forsake you."*
> *Deuteronomy 31:6 NIV*

I AM
HIGHLY BLESSED
AND
UNBELIEVABLY
VALUABLE.

—Shana Danielle

FOUR

Rise

"One of the lessons that I grew up with was to always stay true to yourself
and never let what somebody else says distract you from your goals.
And so when I hear about negative and false attacks,
I really don't invest any energy in them,
because I know who I am."

—Michelle Obama

Shana Danielle

ON THE RISE

I am a black woman
On the rise.
Pushing through, I won't apologize.

Many people tried to keep me down,
But I'm a black woman.
I'mma wear this crown.

Poverty, they thought,
'Cause of this cocoa brown.
Pushin' *me* to the side,
Wantin' *me* to go around.

But I'mma keep going through.
Keep moving forward.
My ancestors taught me
I gotta go onward.

I am a black woman
On the rise.
Pushing through, I won't apologize.

...

Rise

You see
luscious lips
And curvy hips
With legs so long,
But my mind is strong.

I am more than my body.
I am more than my thighs.
I am more than a conqueror.
You can see it in my eyes.

In these sparkling brown eyes,
I just can't hide,
The kindness in my heart,
Not wanting anyone's demise.
Pushing through to reach the sky,
Climbing Jacob's ladder,
I am on the rise.

This majestic skin
Won't have me out, but in.
My God has been too good
And paid it all for my sin.
With Him before me,
I'mma get this win
Not just for me,
But for all my kin.

Shana Danielle

My trust is in, I AM
That I AM.
When I am in trouble,
I know He'll send a Ram.

Jehovah Jirah will lead me to the top.
Never ever am I gonna stop.
Jehovah Jirah will lead me to the top.
Never ever am I gonna stop.

And they ask me
Why?
Because
I am a black woman
On the rise.
I'm pushing through;
    I won't apologize.

Rise

When I was in the seventh grade, I attended Howard M. Phifer Middle School. My English and Language Arts teacher was a petite Italian woman with curly brown hair named Miss Sassano. She was a remarkable teacher who made learning exciting and fun. Little did she know, she was the first to introduce me to the people that started my love for poetry. I've always loved music and creating rhymes. Dancing and rhyming to a beat were my outlets as I bumbled through my adolescent years, but my love for the art of poetry began with Miss Sassano.

Her class exposed me to haikus, odes, limericks, acrostics, Ballads, and narrative poetry. I studied famous poets like Langston Hughes, Nikki Giovanni, and my all-time favorite, Maya Angelou. Maya Angelou's "Virtuous Woman" is a poem that has stuck with me my entire life. It inspired me to write "On the Rise." I wrote a simplified version of it in Miss Sassano's class, which enabled me to win talent shows through high school.

After high school, "On the Rise" meant so much more. Many people told me that this dream I am living couldn't be done. After I gave birth to my oldest son at the tender age of twenty, some close family members said I would not be blessed and even sentenced me to a life on welfare, but I refused to give in to that negativity. I kept pushing myself to keep moving forward. No matter what life threw at me, and boy did life throw me some *doozies*, I resolved to rise.

I challenge you to replace "Black" with your race or ethnicity and feel empowered. Be a Spanish woman on the rise. Be an Asian woman on the rise. Be an Italian woman on the rise. Be a British woman on the rise. Be an American woman on the rise. Just go out and be a woman on the rise. Use this to encourage yourself and others to push through adversity. Regardless of what you may see and/or feel around you, make a resolve to rise.

Rise.

"I can do all things through Christ who strengthens me."
Philippians 4:13 NKJV

I AM UNSTOPPABLE.

— Shana Danielle

PART TWO

I MUST.

I WILL.

I CAN.

Shana Danielle

FOCUS

Focus is a muscle that needs to be strengthened. Just as we get stronger when we lift weights at the gym, our ability to focus will get stronger as we spend time learning to concentrate without distractions. If we are not careful, distractions will ruin our lives before we know it.

To strengthen our focus, we need to clear our heads of all other worries, stressors, and concerns in our lives. Change the scenery. Go to a location that allows the most productivity. Play instrumental music; it can help set the atmosphere, making it conducive for us to accomplish our goals. When another task pops into our heads, we should write it down and move on.

Unplugging from technology for at least thirty minutes can also help us build our ability to focus. When on the computer for a purpose, log out of emails and social media. Place the phone on airplane mode and turn off notifications. In today's society, technology can be the biggest distraction.

Having technology at our fingertips allows us to constantly switch between TV, email, apps, and games without finishing the task we initially started. Too much unfocused time creates the inability to concentrate. We think we are multitasking and in control of what we focus on, but the opposite is true. We need to realize the impact distractions are having on our lives.

Today, many people feel obligated to respond to everything, but not everything requires a reaction. Sometimes our reaction needs to be "be still." So many lives could be saved if we did not feel compelled to respond to every notification while driving. We must deal with our focus deficiency and easy distractibility. It may take some time, but it is imperative that we learn how to live in the moment.

> Success and failure are directly linked to
> our mental strength in focusing.
> You want to achieve your goals and learn new things?
> You want to be successful at work or lose weight?
> You want to be happy?
> You want to conquer anxiety?
> Then you must exercise your ability to focus.
> Place a higher value on your time. You
> deserve joy, peace, and success.

I challenge you to be well rested, think positive thoughts, and minimize people's access to you. Do this, and I guarantee you will find yourself on the pathway to success. It is hard to remain focused when we are worrying about the past or stressing about the future. It is important we remain present in the present. The past cannot be changed, and the future has yet to happen, but today, we can make a difference in our present if we focus.

> Focused people are happy people.

Shana Danielle

I will remain present in the PRESENT.

—Shana Danielle

FIVE

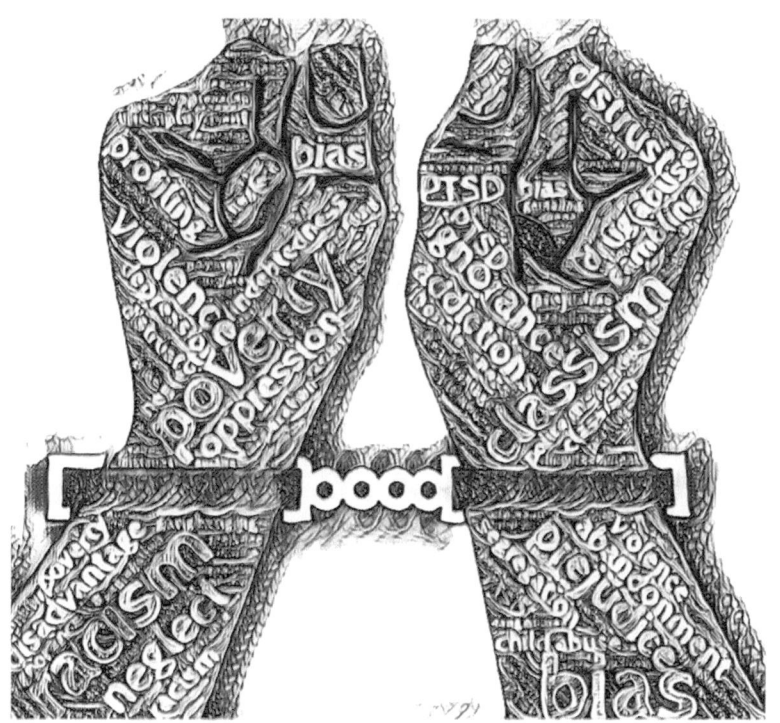

"For to be free is not merely to cast off one's chains, but to live in a way that respects and enhances the freedom of others."

—Nelson Mandela

Shana Danielle

Four Hundred Years

Martin Luther King,
Malcolm X,
Rosa Parks,
Paved the way for respect.

Nicki Minaj,
Lil' Wayne,
Drake,
Boy, how things have changed.

Four hundred years ago,
We were dragged across the ocean blue.
Our captors had to divide us
Or else they would be screwed.

Our numbers were high
and we could overpower
them.
So, they chose to devour
Our
Language, Culture, Heritage.
Our,
Men, Women, Children.
Our,
Strength, Hope, Religion.
And caged us, like a carrier pigeon.

Rise

Four hundred years later,
The division still lingers
Like the effects of a secret
Dropped on Jerry Springer.

Light-skinned were in the house.
Dark-skinned stayed out.
Now,
Light skins on the big screen,
And the covers of magazines.
While
Dark skins are barely lucky,
to get a B-movie scene.

That mentality was taught to keep us apart.
In their eyes we are black,
Doesn't really matter
Light or dark.

Four hundred years ago,
White folks told *knee grows*
Not to read books.
Four hundred years later,
Knee grows tellin' other
Knee grows
not to read 'cause it looks
Dumb.

Shana Danielle

Listen to how you sound.
My people, why we gotta bring our own down?

Nonsense like,
"It's not cool to go to school."
"Getting an education is for fools."
"Bump class, man. How many girls can you pull?"
"Girls, use your jewel, not your mind, as a tool."

It was during the slave trade
White folks began to degrade,
Our ancestors and now *WE*,
Don't know how to behave.

They made our ancestors think *they* were worthless
And now *WE* believe this absurdness.
Treated worse than animals,
We don't deserve this,
But we have to change our thinking if we want to reverse it.

Back,
To when we were Kings and Queens.
Creating lands of Hopes and Dreams.
We ruled the land of Nubia,
Also named Kush.
Now Kush is just something to smoke,
Turning our mind into mush.

My people,
I'm tired of seeing us on the news.

Rise

Hear our Emergency alarm.
Stop pressin' snooze.

Even down to the judicial system of today,
It reminds me of the Jim Crow from yesterday.
Jim Crow Laws enslaved us even though we were free.
And the Judicial system keeps us revolving in captivity.

But we can't keep blaming
Someone else for our problems.
We gotta start new habits,
If we want to resolve them.

Why do you and your enemy
Share the same shade of skin?
We need to lift each other up,
As if they were our kin.

How about we start paying attention in class.
Follow me while I break down this math.

Shana Danielle

Four hundred years ago,
They added us to a new county,
And subtracted our identity,
Multiplied their money,
And divided our family.

Four hundred years later,
They added drugs, creating thugs,
And yet that *still* multiplied their funds.
Subtracted fathers and mothers
And yet,
We are <u>still</u> divided from each other.

Stop running around saying, "I'm on one."
When you need to be takin' care of your son.
Asking questions like, "Where that loud?"
Instead of getting high, how about we reach for the clouds?

I have a dream that one day,
Our kids will go to school in peace.
Without fears or worries
Of being harassed by police.

I have a dream that one day,
If we have to be detained,
It will happen without
Our airways being restrained.

I have a dream that one day,
Our sons will be able to take a jog.

Rise

Without fears of being hunted,
Rest In Peace to Ahmad.

I have a dream that one day,
Our people will be proud to excel in education
Without being the first,
Or only, in their generation.

I have a dream that we will come together,
And help each other in good or bad weather.
But how can we protect our future women and children,
When many of our men are dead or in prison?

My people,
We need to come together and make amends.
This Four hundred-year cycle needs to end.

RETRAIN

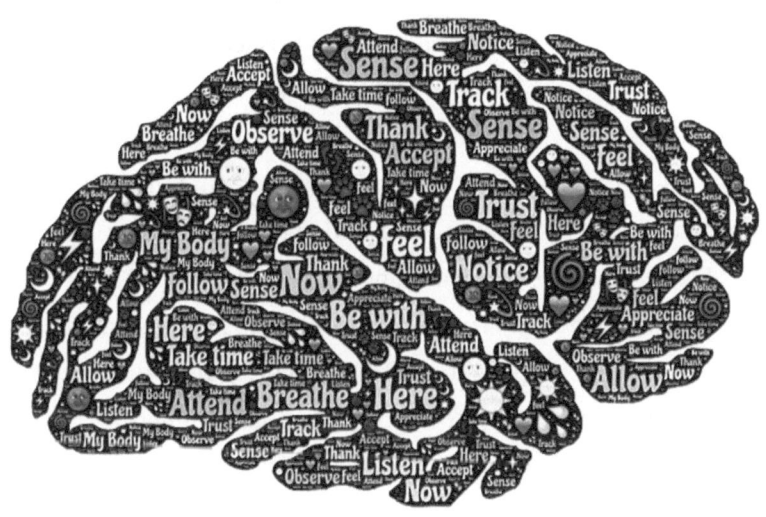

YOUR BRAIN

—Shana Danielle

Rise

It has been said that if you can change your thinking, you can change your life. I firmly believe that. It took years for fruits of the Spirit to resonate with me, and in some, I am still growing. However, love, joy, peace, patience, kindness, goodness, faithfulness, gentleness, and self-control are all meant to be ours.

I am genuinely hurt when I see young people killed over ridiculous things like clothing or respect. While employed as a correctional officer, I would sometimes hear some of the older men talking about their regrets and how they wished they could change things, how they wished they could inspire the youth to not make the same mistakes they did. However, it is extremely difficult and almost impossible to have a substantial impact from behind the wall. Sadly, for some youth, it seems that being behind the wall is on their bucket list. That is, until they are there and reality sets in.

I am also genuinely hurt to see people who look like me getting killed unjustly by people who are nothing more than civilians in blue; who made a solemn promise to protect and serve, simply because of the complexion of their skin. As an African-American wife and mother with experience in law enforcement, these social injustices are exceptionally hard. The lives lost could have been any of my loved ones. The actions of a few bad apples cause a mass distrust for many. We need to be able to trust our law enforcement officers to uphold the law and see that people get their day in court.

I pray every day for my husband and children, especially my sons. The heart broken mothers on the news confirm I am not the only wife and mother who prays a prayer like this:

> God, please send your angels to surround and protect my family from dangers seen and unseen.

Keep Your mighty hand around my husband and children, guarding them from the evil forces that will misjudge them.

Protect their mind from thinking they are all alike. Strengthen their ability to walk in peace, giving no room for bitterness to grow. Bless them with spiritual discernment for making the best decisions at all times.

Bring to their knowledge the truth that they are the Righteousness of Christ and the catalysts for healing, putting our country on the pathway to peace and reconciliation.

God, please give me the desires of my heart. You said in Your Word, "No weapon formed against us will prosper." Please bring my family home safely. Do not allow them to die prematurely, but allow them to live a long life, full of joy, fulfilling their purpose.

In Jesus name, Amen.

    I am a lover and a worshipper of Christ, and I believe in the power of prayer. However, I realize racism cannot be simply prayed away. If we are to rid our society of systemic racism, we must all resolve to dismantle racist beliefs and behaviors. We need to do this as if all our children's lives depend on it; mine do. Faith without works is dead, so we must get to work.
    I challenge everyone, especially my Caucasian allies, to teach

Rise

their own families, friends, and young children more than *tolerance*. I challenge you to teach compassion. I challenge you to embrace self-love, while simultaneously embracing the beauty our differences create when we work together. I challenge you to refuse to remain silent when you witness racist actions or statements. Speak up and maintain your stand! We must be the change we seek!

I challenge you to make a difference in someone else's life today. Volunteer, read a book to at-risk youth at your local community center or school. Start a program like Toys for Tots that operates throughout the year instead of just during the holidays. At-risk youth need encouragement all the time. I emphasize the youth because they are the future generation, and they are capable of succeeding in life without going through unnecessary trials and tribulations, with our help.

Go make a difference in the world.

Rise.

> "Today I have given you the choice between life and death, between blessings and curses. Now I call on heaven and earth to witness the choice you make. Oh, that you would choose life, so that you and your descendants might live!"
> **Deuteronomy 30:19 NLT**

Shana Danielle

I CAN ACHIEVE GREATNESS.

—Shana Danielle

SIX

"I can accept failure.

Everyone fails at something.

But I can't accept **not trying**."

—Michael Jordan

Shana Danielle

SUCCESS

What is success?
Is it becoming who
Society says you should be?
Or is it ruling lands,
Like a Queen or a King?
Could it be … What your status is?
Mr. or Mrs.?
Doctor or Lawyer?
Senator?
President?

Or
Is it that young girl who got pregnant
At the tender age of sixteen
And
Her entire family
Not even supporting,
But promoting,
Resorting to aborting?

She went through many highs and lows,
Had some friends that turned to foes.
But like a Phoenix, up she rose,
And birthed a son. Welp, here it goes.

She got off of welfare and earned her diploma,
Left that small town down in Oklahoma.

Rise

Was blessed to land a good career,
<u>Strangers</u> gave the **biggest** cheer.
She was blessed again with a three-story house.
While others rented or whined,

        "Maaaah!
           Stop coming in unannounced."

So
What is success?
Is it
How many cars you have
Or
How many houses your money can buy?
Is it
How many followers you got on the *Gram*
Or
How many times you said, *"Thank you, ma'am"*?

Or
Is it that little boy
Who got involved with the wrong crowd
And
Did a bid for some things
That didn't make his momma proud?

Man!
She did the best she could, without his father around.

But
Then that little boy got out

And got a *legit* sales job,
Perfected his craft,
No longer a slob.

To be a CEO,
He was anointed and appointed.
He became the one
Providing many with employment.
That boy turned into a man that day.
In the middle of nowhere,
He found his way.

Hmmm…
So,
What is the true definition of success?
It is
Overcoming obstacles,
Despite the weight of stress;
Becoming who everyone said you couldn't,
And doing it with finesse.
Reaching and teaching others,
To become their very best.

Yes!
In the world,
It is a hard thing to achieve success.
But it is attainable
To anyone
Who will persevere

Rise

And fight to overcome.
So, no matter who you are,
Or where you are from—
Detroit, Chicago, B-More, Harlem,
Queens, Brooklyn, Bronx, or Compton—
And even if you're from (as the media mentioned),
Poor
Most Dangerous
Ghetto
Camden.

Rise Up!
Against the chains meant to keep you bound
And **Rise Up!**
Against corruption meant to hold you down.
Rise Up!
Despite the stereotypes.
And **Rise Up** to conquer with all your might!

Don't give in
To what society wants.
You are in the system,
And your memories haunt-

Haunt you in your dreams
Of all you could have achieved
If only you would have
Just done the right thing.

Shana Danielle

So next time you get tempted to do something that's not right,
Rise up to the test because you all are bright.

And even if jailin'
Is all you know how to do,
It is not too late,
Even for you.
So,
Share what you learned from your past,
And
We can all be great at last.
Pay it forward
Put it to the test.
We can **ALL** achieve
Success.

"Do the best you can until you know better. Then when you know better, **do better.**"

— Maya Angelou

Shana Danielle

I WILL CONTROL MY THOUGHTS!

— Shana Danielle

Rise

Thoughts
Before you catch a feeling,
You'll always catch a thought.
Anxiety then attacks,
Something you should have never caught.

> Be careful of your thoughts;
> Your thoughts become your life.
> Pure thoughts, they're good,
> Bad thoughts become a knife

>> To cut you off from purpose
>> And cut your destiny–
>> Cut away your joy,
>> And destroy your sanity.

Shana Danielle

My thoughts control my **destiny.** I am destined for great things.

—Shana Danielle

Rise

I was a person who knew God but thought I knew best. I would never admit it out loud, or to myself for that matter, but I did things the way I wanted to do them. I was interested in being who He called me to be, but not committed. I *turnt up* in the clubs every single night. I went to college, and then I dropped out while on a full academic scholarship. Yeah, I know what you're thinking, especially if you have student loans, but I was chasing money. I was later married, cheated on, abused, used, and divorced.

The process of learning how to be in the world but not of the world has been a challenging journey. There are some experiences I sometimes wish **never** happened. I have come to accept that had I not gone through those situations, I would not rely on God like I do today. My shortcomings and series of unfortunate events did not matter when I rededicated my life to Christ. I found my purpose, and then success finally happened in my life.

I was blessed with the opportunity to work in a re-entry program for individuals returning to society after incarceration. This program connected inmates with the services, which enabled them to be successful and reduced recidivism. While being part of this awesome mission, I had the ability to witness people make impossible situations work for their good. I've witnessed people who were strung out on drugs and lost their children become clean and gain their families back. I have observed individuals who spent over twenty years in and out of incarceration start and keep their own businesses.

I know without a shadow of a doubt that you were born to fulfill your purpose in life. However, in order to do so, you need to surround yourself with people who are going to encourage you and push you to become the best version of yourself. Do not let a bad mistake define you. Do not let the guilt from an awful decision keep you in bondage. It is never too late to change the trajectory of your life. I challenge you to let it go, live with a purpose and be successful.

Rise.

> *"Jesus looked at them and said, 'With man this is impossible, but with God all things are possible.'"*
> *Matthew 19:26 NIV*

Do NOT
listen to the
CRITICS!
STAY FOCUSED!

—Shana Danielle

SEVEN

"Every time you state what you want or believe, you're the first to hear it. It's a message to both you and others about what you think is possible. Don't put a ceiling on yourself."
—Oprah Winfrey

Shana Danielle

TIME

Time can be very kind to you,
But beware of the time.
It can *ah ah chooo*.

Blow away in the breeze,
With the birds and the bees.
Time only guarantees
it will never freeze.

So today, go seize.
Cross all your T's.
Maybe it's just me and
My idiosyncrasies.

But I suggest you watch it
Like the money in your pocket
Or the clothes in your closet
'Cause you can never stop it.

Our Master's plan
Since time began
Was to understand,
Not be lost in the sand.

Tick. Tock.
Tick. Tock.
Tick. Tock.

Rise

Boom!

Time is precious,
Not something to waste.
What you do with your time
can never be erased.

Once it's gone, it's gone.
You can never get it back.
Time is valuable,
Like diamonds that are black.

Time is priceless,
Yet people choose to waste it.
They dwell on the past,
They rearview racin'.

There's a shortage of time
So many praise YOLO.
But don't take it too literally,
And copy Drake's *dough flow.*

Yes, it is true,
You only live once.
But that doesn't mean to live
Like you're a dummy stunt.
This recording is live,
You're not a stunt *dummy.*
It's not Hollywood,
Livin' for the love of money.

Tick. Tick.
    Tick. Tick.
        Tick. Tick.
            BOOM!

Run away.
    Run away.
        Run away.
            VROOM!

Can't hold it.
Can't catch it.
No credit.
Just debit.

They say time is money
And money is time.
But make time for your family;
They shouldn't wait in line.

Take the time to smell the tulips,
    Watch the birds fly.
Before your very eyes,
    Time
        Will
            Pass
                You …
                    BYE.

Rise

At the time of writing the introduction, I had wasted seven years of my life not being the best version of myself. If I am completely transparent, it was probably longer, but my desire to publish poetry was my point of reference. I could have been pouring out more positivity during that time and filling myself up with the Word to be more prepared for the trials and tribulations of life. However, I did not have a full appreciation of time's worth.

In 2017, I lost my father and had a reality shock. He was a five-time cancer survivor who had nine lives and always found a way to bounce back stronger each time. He bounced back from prostate cancer, lung cancer, bladder cancer, throat cancer, and voice box cancer, all while caring for his mother, Caroline Davis, who lived nine months beyond his death, passing away in 2018 at the young age of one hundred and four. That last time battling cancer, my father was extremely ill, recovery not in sight; although I knew his death was coming, I still was not prepared for the thirst and desire to have more time.

We need to cherish time. I felt compelled to write this book when the COVID-19 pandemic opened the world's eyes to time's true value. Weddings were cancelled, travel plans postponed, graduations were virtual, and birthdays were celebrated alone. Sweet, bright-eyed, beautiful babies were born without the welcoming and closeness of family. And sadly, many people lost their loved ones, and it felt premature.

We do not know the minute or the hour our time will end on this earth. Some choose to sit around and waste their gift of time, never fulfilling their purpose. They miss their calling by living in the past, allowing the hurt, guilt, and shame of previous mistakes to consume them in the present. Others seem to freely throw their time away on the philosophy that you only live once (YOLO). Many people live today as if there is no tomorrow. Being drunk, high, promiscuous, or shopping until their accounts are empty drives their existence.

Time is such a precious experience.
If you still have breath in your lungs,
it is never too late to stop existing and start living.
Place a higher value on the gift of time.

Rise!

> "For everything there is a season, a time for every activity under heaven."
> Ecclesiastes 3:1 NLT

I AM DETERMINED TO MAKE THE MOST OF MY TIME!

— Shana Danielle

EIGHT

"If you are fortunate to have opportunity, it is your duty to make sure other people have those opportunities as well."

– Kamala Harris

Shana Danielle

SHOES

Sneakers.
High Heels.
Open Toes.
Espadrilles.
Sandals.

There are many different kinds of shoes—
Cowboy boots, pumps, so many to choose.
Flats, Mary Janes, loafers, and flip-flops,
Wedges, gladiators, stilettos, and Crocs.

Everyone has a different style they like.
Some you may wear, other shoes are solely their type.
In basketball you Criss Cross with Mikes,
Or lace up Sauconys when you ride your bike.

Sling Backs.
High Tops.
Oxfords.
Expensive.
Stilettos.

Some travel Bloomingdale's.
Some stuck in the jails.
Some make them an obsession.
Some try to take them to heaven.

Rise

Be mindful before you judge,
Based off the shoes on someone's feet.
Because you don't know all the roadways
Those shoes had to meet.

Not everyone can rock Gucci, Louis, and Prada.
Some wear out *Bo-Bos* as long as they gotta,
Find a *hand-me*-down from someone else,
Not everyone's had a silver spoon dealt.

Be:
Selfless.
Helpful.
Open-Minded.
Empathetic.
Sensitive.

Many walk around and pray for something to give,
Trying to figure out the right way to live.
Don't take the shoes you wear for granted
Because in the blink of an eye, they can be recanted.

Shoes take us here, there, and everywhere.
Some people don't have any; if you have extra, share.
One day your Jordans could vanish into thin air,
And then be replaced with a no-name pair.

Some people preach survival of the fittest,
And if you have no shoes, then that's your business.
But the call on our lives is for us to finish

Shana Danielle

Happily, soon you'll see, 'Cause I'm a witness.
So be

Supportive.
Humble.
Open.
Encouraging and
Share.

One day you may have
No shoes to wear.

I am BLESSED

to BE a BLESSING

Shana Danielle

"Try walking a mile in my shoes" is a phrase that many people will use when they feel condemned by those around them. Feeling judged is never an enjoyable experience, but that explains the complete phrase, "**Before** *you judge someone*, walk a mile in their shoes."

I am not sure how, as a society, we have become so judgmental, but our preconceptions have hindered us from rising to our fullest potential. We need to resolve to meet people where they are and stop judging the symptoms (their reactions), while ignoring the underlying illness, which is the bigger problem. When we tell people what they should be doing, we leave them feeling overwhelmed, intimidated, and frustrated. Our desires and passions fit our lives, not necessarily everyone else's.

It is common in this generation, just as in other generations, to constantly pass judgment on others, whether intentional or not; we are all guilty of it from time to time. However, not every judgment is negative. If you saw someone giving a homeless person food, you would believe they had a good heart. Judging only becomes problematic when we make unnecessary, hurtful, or unfair judgments with little proof.

For example, when a girl births a child at an early age, people tend to judge or assume that she is promiscuous. They tend to treat the young lady as if she is a harlot and look at her with such contempt and scrutiny. However, what if she had her innocence snatched unwillingly and the child was a result of something beyond her control?

Or how about a person who holds the line up at the grocery store using W.I.C. (Women, Infants, and Children) checks? Some would believe they are lazy and reaping the benefits from others' hard-earned dollars. Many would never consider that this person had a car accident that almost took their life or believe the EMTs declared

Rise

this person dead on arrival. This is a true story of a close friend of mine, and it was only by the Grace of God that my friend is alive today. The accident initially left my friend unable to work, but they did their best to care for the family.

When we look at others and find them "*less than*" because they are *less like us* than we want them to be, we are judging people. As a society, we need to have more empathy and less sympathy. We just need to stop and think about what it is we are truly judging and if it really matters in the long run, whatever the issue may be.

I was married, and it ended in divorce rather quickly. Many people judged me. The judgements evolved when I remarried five years later. What people did not know was that I dealt with being cheated on repeatedly and assaulted in the marriage; he was convicted on charges after the domestic violence happened. People did not know I was trying to find a way for my children to be cared for so I could disappear and know they would be okay ... but God!

God delivered me through all that, and I now have peace. My ex-husband and I have been able to work through our differences and work together in the best interest of our child. I am also happily remarried, and my marriage this go-round is closer together and closer to God than I could ever imagine. It didn't start out that way, and we've had our fair share of challenges to overcome, but with God, all things are possible.

My husband and I went from binge watching shows on Netflix to binge watching sermons on YouTube. While we were on quarantine during the COVID-19 epidemic, we began watching sermons from our home church, El Bethel Community Cathedral in Palymra, NJ, pastored by Bishop Joseph Roberts, Jr. That led to us watching sermons from churches across the nation, including Pastor Michael Todd of Transformation Church (Tulsa, OK), Pastor John Gray from Relentless

Church (Greenville, SC), Pastor Stevin Furtick from Elevation Church (Charlotte, NC) and countless others who ministered to our spirits.

On this journey, we have learned to live by a motto of being "**AMP**ed." My husband and I are determined to achieve more for our lives. As we *achieve more*, we want to be a blessing to others, not just financially, but also through comforting, encouraging, and *motivating others* to live life to its fullest potential. We believe that as we **achieve more**, and in turn **motivate others** to succeed, we can all **prosper together** to make the world a better place.

I challenge you to be more "**AMP**ed" in your life. Do not focus so much on what others have or do not have. Focus on the journey in front of you. While on your journey, if you can be a blessing and help someone else, just do it. Let us all prosper together.

Rise.

> "Refuse to be a critic full of bias toward others, and judgment will not be passed on you. ² For you'll be judged by the same standard that you've used to judge others. The measurement you use on them will be used on you. ³ Why would you focus on the flaw in someone else's life and yet fail to notice the glaring flaws of your own? ⁴ How could you say to your friend, 'Let me show you where you're wrong,' when you're guilty of even more? ⁵ You're being hypercritical and a hypocrite! First acknowledge your own 'blind spots' and deal with them, and then you'll be capable of dealing with the 'blind spot' of your friend."
> Matthew 7:1-5 TPT

I WILL **Achieve** more.

I WILL **Motivate** others.

WE WILL **Prosper** together.

I WILL BE **AMPED**!

—Shana Danielle

PART THREE

Rise

Let

It

Go.

Shana Danielle

BE VULNERABLE

Vulnerability!
The greatest measure of courage.
It requires us to pour out from the most valuable places deep inside ourselves.
Vulnerability is a level of authenticity unable to be achieved without an unbelievable amount of strength and courage. To be vulnerable is to expose that which is most precious to us,
allowing our deepest thoughts, challenges, feelings, and weaknesses to be scrutinized by others.
When we are vulnerable, we risk the possibility of attack or harm, physically or emotionally.

Vulnerability!
It is empowering.
It allows us the opportunity to overcome our fears and anxiety. When we are open to criticism or rejection, we are also open to growth, strength, and change.
Opportunities arise that never could happen without overcoming the fears that hindered our advancement in life.
We experience fear when we are not in control of a situation but want to manipulate the result to fit our desires. To be vulnerable is to expose our fears *on purpose* so that we may have a chance to live *with purpose.*

Vulnerability!
Free yourself.

Rise

Vulnerability allows us to experience new things, create new relationships and build new networks.

I challenge you to conquer your fears, to push through the anxiety and recognize overcoming your fears will set you free. Be vulnerable and allow yourself the opportunity to do something you've always wanted to do but permitted fear to hinder you. Vulnerability is risky but vital.

Vulnerability can allow us to rise.

Shana Danielle

IT'S OKAY TO BE VULNERABLE. VULNERABILITY MAKES YOU POWERFUL!

—Shana Danielle

NINE

"It doesn't matter how rich or poor a person is, what gender or social class, or how much fame or education she possesses. Verbal, mental, and physical abuse can happen to anyone. It doesn't matter what a woman's ethnicity is because the only distinguishing color of abuse is **black-and-blue.**"

— La Toya Jackson

Shana Danielle

BLACK AND BLUE

Black and blue and purple and red,
So many knots and lumps upside my head.

It's my fault; I should have never fed
Into his drama, should have just stayed in bed.
Maybe I should have pretended to be dead
While he tore my insides and soul to shreds.

But instead, I had to talk back,
Which made him angry and then he attacked,
But I'll never tell my family … On him I'll never rat.
I'll just cover up these bruises with some Cover Girl and MAC.

Black and blue and purple and red,
So many knots and lumps upside my head.

Sometimes I want my temple pierced with lead
If it means the end of my eternal dread.
He says he loves me, so I lightly tread,
Make sure to obey every word he's said.
If I try to escape, there won't be enough meds
To change me back from being undead.

But at times, he can be so sweet,
Make me feel like treasure. I know he won't cheat.
The light switches on, and it's me he beats.
It only happens when he and the forty meet,

Rise

Or if I forget to change the bed sheets.
This life I live, it's on repeat.
Repeat. Repeat.
Repeat.

Black and blue and purple and red,
Today he gave roses, not lumps on my head.

"Baby, please," he begged and pled.
I know he's sorry; it just went unsaid.
I knew he'd change and one day we'd wed.
Some said leave and I almost sped
Away from him, but I was misled.

Who am I fooling? I'm on a road that he paves,
Leading me straight to my six-foot grave.
Perpetual torment, I am enslaved.
Where is this Savior? Does He save?

I need to love myself, not tomorrow, today
Or eventually the final price I will pay.
I could try God. Tomorrow's the day.
His empire seems so far away.

Red and blue and purple and black.
Roses and lilies they bring, and lilacs.
My mom feels like she was hit with a Mack
As she wipes her tears delicately and sits back.

Shana Danielle

I was always told someone else would love me.
Eve said love was blind, but he seemed too lovely.
While sipping your tea, you all saw this coming.
But I am finally free. The harps are strumming.

Today, they send roses to my hole in the earth.
They cover my casket with soil and dirt.
Ashes to ashes. I no longer hurt.
Dust to dust. Rest in peace on a shirt.

Black and white and red and brown,
Doesn't really matter, your background.
I beg you to use my life as an example.
Domestic violence is not something you need to sample.

If you or someone you know is experiencing or could potentially be suffering from abuse, please call the National Domestic Violence Hotline at 1-800-799-SAFE. That's 1-800-799-7233. Or Safe Horizon at 1-800-621-HOPE. That's 1-800-621-4673

If you or someone you know is in immediate danger or having a medical emergency, call 911.

Everyone has a right to live violence free. Domestic violence rarely starts out in a full-blown rage episode. It often begins with subtle verbal abuse or criticism, usually about physical appearance or the inability to do anything right. It then frequently progresses to isolation of the victim. If an abuser can separate an individual from their family and friends, they have a higher probability of succeeding in controlling the victim with their threats. After threats, physical and sexual abuse are the next step in the sad progression of domestic violence.

The heart-breaking reality for many victims is not knowing how to escape. Once a person is trapped with an abuser, it becomes extremely difficult to reach out for help. Many find themselves remaining in an abusive situation because of the uncertainty and unknowns in leaving. Where will they go? Who will they live with? What if the abuser finds them? Who will love them?

If you are reading this page and you are being subjected to abuse, know you do not have to be a victim. "Black and Blue" does not have to be the end for your life. You can be a survivor. Even if you have children, you and your children can outlive your current circumstance. You can be a living testimony to encourage the next victim and let them know "abuse is no excuse."

With handprint bruises embedded around your neck, I urge you to muster up the strength and courage to flee. I know someone did not believe you. They enabled your abuser by accusing you of making it up. With that cut on your swollen lip, escape, and keep telling your story. There is support for you. There are people who will love you. Someone will believe you. **You are amazing and deserve to be loved.**

To any abuser reading, it is important you understand it is not too late for you to turn your life over to God. God can help you overcome this demonic spirit. He can help you bind it and send it back to the pits of hell. I employ you to seek wise counsel in resolving issues that led to you becoming an abuser. Maybe you were abused and have locked it away deep, where no one can find it. I challenge you to expose it and heal from your pain.

Hurt people hurt people. Everyone needs healing in one area or another. All have sinned and fallen short of the Glory of God. Thanks to His Grace, we can all be saved. Abusers and victims must understand you cannot do this on your own. I challenge you to love yourself. I have personally witnessed someone turn into the worst kind of abuser you could imagine while under the influence of drugs and alcohol. This person turned their life over to Christ and, through God's love, evolved into a philanthropist.

I am not encouraging anyone to remain with an abuser in hopes of them becoming better. Remaining in an unhealthy environment is not beneficial for your safety, growth, and healing. I am encouraging both victims and abusers to try Jesus, not half steppin', but with your whole heart. As you get closer with Him and love Him, you will learn to love yourself. The sad truth that many will not admit is that both victims and abusers have minimal love for themselves. If you do not genuinely love yourself, you cannot possibly begin to love someone else.

Have faith in God to transform and renew your heart, but also know faith without works is dead. Counseling is a major part of healing, but it is a taboo topic in many households. I find it odd that we can take our cars to get an oil change, refill the gas tank, and get a weekly wash, yet we will not seek a mental health professional to assist us in the healing of our mind and emotions.

My daughter broke two bones in her right forearm while doing cartwheels at the tender age of five. I did not take her in the house to say a prayer then keep it moving. My husband and I rushed her to the hospital so she could get treated and heal properly. I prayed the doctors were guided by the Holy Spirit and trusted God would allow her to recover fully, but I did not just leave it all in prayer, I had to do some work.

When people have scars from abuse, relationship issues (family, friends, spouse, etc.) or wounds causing depression, we must stop advising them to simply pray about it. We need to encourage them to pray, and pray in agreement with them, to find a professional to aid in their healing.

Healing is not an overnight process. When my daughter broke her arm, she was in a hard cast for six weeks, a brace for five months and had at least five follow-up appointments. I challenge you to be honest with yourself. Do not run from your feelings; embrace them. And if you discover there is an area in which you need healing, seek the counseling you need. Do not rush your healing, take your time with a professional, and if the first professional is not a good fit, try again. If we are not willing to do the work, we will continue to get the same results.

I challenge everyone to check on friends and family you have not heard from in a while. When you see someone being abused or being the abuser, do not remain silent. Silence enables the vicious cycle of violence to continue. Regardless of how minuscule the abuse seems, be an advocate in ending the cycle. We can all make a difference if we work together.

Rise.

"Jesus replied, 'You must love the Lord your God with all your heart, all your soul, and all your mind.' This is the first and greatest commandment. A second is equally important: 'Love your neighbor as yourself.'"
Matthew 22:37-39 NLT

I WILL MAKE IT!
I AM STRONG!

—Shana Danielle

"Abusers—they'll manipulate, and they'll lie to you. And when you no longer give them that power, they'll try to manipulate your family or the people close to you instead. Abusers want everyone to hate you just as much as they do. It's sick. Their lack of morals and integrity is sick. The amount of hate they harbor in their hearts is sick, as are their psychopathic or sociopathic traits."

— LaTasha "Tacha B." Braxton

Rise

Racing

At three a.m. when you can't rest
Your thoughts race.
You feel depressed.
Lonely.
Broken.
Battered.
Bruised.

Feel the power and love
In Him. He wants you loosed.

Shana Danielle

I AM LOVED!
I HAVE PEACE!

-Shana Danielle

TEN

"How far you go in life depends on your being tender with the young, compassionate with the aged, sympathetic with the striving, and tolerant of the weak and strong. Because someday in your life you will have been all of these."

– George Washington Carver

Shana Danielle

THE FALL

(Deep sigh)

Got my bag, Now I can cook my dope.
I feel euphoria, like a captain on his boat.

I love–no–I lust the process of mixing.
Anxious, heart pounding, mind racing, I'm tripping.

I fill the syringe and my body starts to cringe.
I need it, gotta have it, like a bulimic to binge.

Now I search for a vein, like a lion hunts her prey.
I gotta find it soon. My body seems to decay.

Yes! Red! I finally boot it.
Thumb at the top, I push it and shoot it.
I feel it traveling through my veins, like a fish through the sea.
Head to toe, oh so warm, my body tingling.

Psychedelic horse ride, I'm in a Twilight Zone.
My high is like an orgasm. I'm the Queen on her throne.
Now, sit back and let me share this true story:
The rise, the fall, drama you see on Maury.

. . .

Rise

It started at a party.
I was only seventeen
Having innocent fun with friends,
When *Matega* entered the scene.

He told me don't worry,
You won't get addicted.
It's like *Mary Jane*;
You'll only feel a little twisted.

Little did I know
He wanted to make me his whore
So he could pimp me out;
I'd be his walking store.

Having sex to get high,
Got high so I wouldn't cry.
Thinking about my problems
Made me wish I'd just die.

Twenty two bags a day,
I am now twenty one.
I get locked up
And find out I'm having a son.

Or daughter?
How could this happen to me?
Me? A mommy?
Naw, I'm a loner. I roam free.

Shana Danielle

C/Os take me to the hospital,
And nurses can't get an I.V.
I guess it's too many track lines,
No veins left to see.

Then they tell me I'm positive—
HIV.
This mess only happens in movies
Or MTV.

...

What happened to the smart schoolgirl,
The girl next door,
The one who loved education,
Always yearning for more?

I had many friends,
My whole family loved me.
I'd dreamed of a big house,
A white fence and a puppy.

Beautiful smile.
Even, smooth skin.
Loved and desired,
Both out and in.
I was a Beauty Queen,
No marks, no scars.
    Now I no longer care;
    I stand outside of bars.

Rise

No longer picky
Of which man could stick me
As long was the money,
Was enough to fix me.

I'm living in abandoned houses,
Back alleys in the streets.
H is no longer a high;
It's a disease.

Nausea, diarrhea, I got a monkey on my back.
Not eating, not sleeping, shakes, aches and all that.
My family disowns me,
I walk the street lonely.
I'm an ugly junkie.
Heroin controls me.

And then, when I see a dirty pig,
I already know what it is.
He takes me, rapes me,
Now I'm covered in his jizz.
But none of that matters,
When I get my bags,
D-Block will temporarily make me
Forget all the bad.

...

Shana Danielle

Now, as I look at my body,
I have nowhere else to hit.
So I stare in the shattered mirror,
Thinking I'll see something I missed.

And then a light bulb goes off,
But I say, "No! I can't do this."
Then *Diesel* tells me, "Try it.
I'm sure you won't miss."

So I grit my teeth
And place my hand on my neck.
I can feel my aorta pumping,
Waiting for the needle's peck.

Prick!!
I think the color was too dark brown.
Now I am feeling too dizzy.
The room is spinning around.

I stumble.
I stagger.
I trip,
And I fall.
This time, there's no one around for me to call.

Thump!

. . .

Rise

Blacking out,
Is nothing new to me.
You'd think with all the times I overdosed,
Recovery would have come through to me.
But this time, it's just me and the *D*.
At least I won't die,
Kicking,
On E.

If you or a loved one has an addiction or is in need of some guidance and support with substance abuse issues, please call the Substance Abuse and Mental Health Service Administration Hotline at 1-800-799-HELP. That's 1-800-799-4357.

If you or someone you know is in immediate danger or having a medical emergency, call 911.

Addiction is a very complex disorder, and it places a major strain on the people surrounding the addict. The closer the relationship, the greater the strain and desire for the addict to just get sober. Some would believe once an individual goes to rehab and comes home, all their problems are immediately resolved, when in actuality this is when the greatest challenge begins.

Individuals in recovery are in the toughest battle of their lives and, without proper support, will fail every time. Sometimes the thought of maintaining a substance-free life is scary, just as trying to live a life free from lying, cheating, or stealing can be overwhelming. People who struggle with addiction often feel ashamed, guilty, and worthless. They have a hard time believing they can have a meaningful life again.

The best way a loved one can help a person struggling with addiction is to become informed. Loved ones should never approach from a place of judgement, but always from a place of love. It is important to try to place yourself in the addict's shoes and imagine how life is for them. Loved ones need to learn about potential triggers, psychological changes, health concerns, and the twelve-step recovery process.

I am no expert in these areas, but while working in the reentry program, I sat in on a lot of recovery meetings and learned a lot. It

Rise

helped me to not be judgmental and learn to have compassion. I've heard the stores firsthand and was surprised to learn many afflicted with addiction started out very successful. On their journey, many became addicted while in unhealthy relationships.

In recovery, healthy relationships are important, and loved ones cannot put all the expectations on the addict to recover. They need to understand they play an integral part in the addict's recovery and also need to assume some responsibility in aiding recovery. Trying to support a loved one struggling with addiction without proper support is impossible. Therapy, exercise, and group activities like yoga and support groups are critical for both the addict and the loved one.

Small support groups are extremely important. There, people find accountability partners, friendships, helpful tips and strategies—imperative tips like the removal of all addictive substances from the home, avoiding events where abuse will occur, creating healthy habits, and finding sober friendships. Learning to manage stress, but also avoiding unnecessary stress, will minimize the chance of relapse.

If you are struggling with drug addiction and feel you have no place to turn, please know you are not alone. While some believe addictions are only bad habits that can be defeated with will power alone, I know it is bigger than you. Addiction can only be defeated with help from the One who created you. This may be a solution that you do not want to face or feel that you are not deserving of, but I promise you, you are loved. If you have tried everything else, try Jesus Christ. He wants you to enjoy a peaceful, blessed life.

To the Christians, please have compassion in your heart and be a reflection of God's love. Sometimes we forget where we've come from and will judge people based on their current or past sins. Kanye West has a song entitled "Hands On," in which he explains how he told people his mission was to serve God and create gospel music. People would then ask him what Christians said to him about his desire to change music genres. He responds by saying Christians were the first to cast judgement on him. He feels the Christians would judge him so badly it would make him feel as if no one loves him. Many people won't even listen to his gospel songs because of his past.

We have to do better in embracing people before they become "holy and sanctified." In recovery, the most valuable resource I've seen people receive is coming to know Jesus. We have to make it easier and be the light in this dark, cold world. It takes a village to not only raise a child, but also to be successful. I challenge all of us to make a difference. I challenge all of us to rise.

Rise.

> "God saved you by his grace when you believed. And you can't take credit for this; it is a gift from God. Salvation is not a reward for the good things we have done, so none of us can boast about it. For we are God's masterpiece. He has created us anew in Christ Jesus, so we can do the good things he planned for us long ago."
> Ephesians 2: 8-10 NLT

After my mess,
I can still
LIVE
my best.

— Shana Danielle

ELEVEN

"Everything negative—pressure, challenges—is all an opportunity for me to rise."

-Kobe Bryant

Shana Danielle

RISE

You can rise.

Yes, it seems you're on the bottom right now.
Making it out, you just don't see how.
But what is a diamond before it is refined?
Coal. Something black and ugly, not even worth a dime.

But then it goes through a metamorphosis,
Like how a caterpillar turns into a butterfly.
There is a reasoning for your suffering,
Although you may not yet understand why.

But you can rise.

Sometimes, the body has to be broken down.
For you to appreciate a smile, you've had to frown.
For you to truly understand what it means to be happy,
There had to be times when you were mad, fanatically.

But that point when you were feeling your lowest,
Is when you build all your strength. It's imperative you notice,
Everything that got you to this point in your life.
To not be here again is going to be a fight.

But you can rise.

Rise

Rise to become everything they said you couldn't be.
Rise to become the person they no longer pity.
From a seed, flowers do grow,
But they must be cared for or their beauty will never show.

Just as a rose, lily, or lilac
Growing out of nothing, that's something. You've got to try that.
The pain that you've felt was never meant to break you
But to take you higher. It was meant to shape you.

You can rise.

Don't let stereotypes keep you oppressed.
Show the world you can do it; give them your best.
But don't do it for them. Do it for you.
No need to sit around singing the blues.

Because you can rise.

Write down your goals and reach for the sky.

Because you can rise.

Shoot for the stars; you've got to aim high.

Because you can rise.

It won't happen on its own. You've got to try.

But you can rise.

Say it:

I can rise.

Say it:

I will rise.

Come on.

Let's all rise.

Rise.

Rise.

Rise.

"Blessed is the one who perseveres under trial because, having stood the test, that person will receive the crown of life that the Lord has promised to those who love him."
James 1:12 NIV

I WILL RISE!

— Shana Danielle

TWELVE

Rise

"I'm just a living witness that you can be an imperfect soldier and still be in the army fighting for God Almighty. Don't you think you got to be perfect 'cause I ain't."

-Steve Harvey

I write to encourage people on all different levels with all kinds of problems and all kinds of passions. Regardless of your background, my desire is never to judge. We all have sinned and fallen short of the Glory of God, but by His Grace we are saved. I hope through *Rise* you can find purpose. I hope through *Rise* you can become healed and motivated.

If you ever doubt that you are called or worthy, look no further than the Grace of God through Jesus. On the journey of writing *Rise*, I became closer with God. As I came closer to its completion, it seemed like every trial and tribulation was thrown my way, but I stayed faithful because God's Word has never turned void in my life.

Please know God has not forgotten you. If it seems like everything is working against you, get closer to Him, and know with God before you, no one can be against you. I need you to believe the best in you; I believe the best in you. You are so amazing and have no reason to be anyone else except yourself. You have greatness inside of you. What you have is what you need.

God can take any situation in your life and it can flourish. Your glitch can become your gift. (Thanks, Charles Metcalf III, creative pastor from Transformation Church.) What the enemy meant for evil in your life, God can turn around for your good.

If you have been wronged by someone, you have to forgive them. Forgiveness is not for them, but for you and your peace. If you do not get the hurt out of your heart, it will turn into bitterness. You must let it go. Speak to your heart and free yourself from resentment.

If this book touched you but you are not saved, meaning you don't know God, I want to take this moment to pray with you, but what is a poetry book without exploring this poetically?

VOICES

Hey you,
You will never make it.
You're not good enough.
You're always gonna fail.
That task is just too tough.

You were made too small.
You were made too fat.
You'll always be poor.
You were made too black.

Every day is a battle,
A battle with my mind.
I struggle just to smile,
Peace is hard to find.

Everyone has it better;
I never get to win.
They all get to be happy;
Their pictures rub it in.

I wish I had someone
Who would truly love me,
But that will never happen
Because I am so ugly.

Shana Danielle

Ugly on the outside.
Ugly deep within.
Messed up too many times.
Enjoyed too many sins.

They said there is a God
To help me and my mess,
But the mess is now too big;
It would cause this God to stress.

Stress about the lies.
Stress about the pride.
Stress about my cries.

…Shhhhh.

Hear a word from the wise.

They said you wouldn't make it.
They said it couldn't be done.
Said you did too many wrong,
God said, *"You've already won."*

When they said that you were worthless,
You entertained their lies.
They meant to break your spirit.
They wanted your demise

And to believe your past
Would keep you an outcast,

Rise

But no abuse can keep you bound.
You are healed 'cause He was slashed.

God wants you in His Kingdom
And to live eternally.
He wants to bring you peace.
He wants to set you free.

Those felonies you committed
And one-night stands can't keep you out.
The adultery and abortion,
He still loves you, never doubt.

Your past, it doesn't matter.
He only wants your heart.
He'll be there in the end
Like he was at the start.

Pride doesn't matter,
Nor your sexuality.
He already paid for that
When he was hung at Calvary.

So come on and try Jesus.
He will lift you up
Out of the pain and the bondage.
Damages He'll cover up.

But you don't know what I've been through;
You don't know what I did.

Shana Danielle

How could Jesus love me?
I did *all* that He forbids.
And if there was a God,
Why do bad things happen?
I lost some of my loved ones…

        Wait, have you seen *The Passion?*

        The Passion of the Christ
        Depicts what Jesus did.
        He did it all for us
        So that we all might live.

        The things in your life,
        That you only see as bad
        Were meant to make you grow,
        Not to keep you sad.

        Through all of the hurt
        And pain you feel,
        You can help someone;
        Others can be healed.

        Share your testimony.
        Your mess becomes a message.
        Through it, you can be healed…

Okay, I have a question.
How can I have a relationship with Jesus?
I think He's the answer

Rise

To give me strength in weakness.

I am glad that you asked.
Pray this prayer with me:
God wants you blessed
And to live eternally.

God,
Thank you for sending Jesus, just for me.
I believe He lived and died to set me free.
Because three days later He rose again,
Please forgive me of all my sins.

Change my life and make me new.
Help me, Lord, to live for You.
I repent and turn from all my ways
And promise to follow you all my days.

If you said this prayer,
I believe you're saved.
Let's rejoice!
I'm glad you prayed.

> "Come to me, all you who are weary and
> burdened, and I will give you rest."
> **Matthew 11:28 NIV**

Shana Danielle

Rise

I LOVE YOU.
IT'S TIME TO RISE!

—Shana Danielle

Acknowledgments

Thanks and glory be to God, my Heavenly Father, who has given His Grace to me. I give much gratitude for all He has blessed me with and for saving me from dangers seen and unseen. All my accomplishments in life have been supported in love and prayer by some awesome people surrounding me.

I thank God for blessing me with this circle of people who love and support me in my endeavors. In the process of getting here, I've made some mistakes, but the foundation I was raised on helped me find my strength in the midst of storms. I would like to take a moment and acknowledge some special people. I could not have done this without the patience, love, discipline, forgiveness, and compassion of my loved ones.

To my husband, Adam Parker, I want to thank you for your love, support, and passionate desire to see me succeed. Your love kept me going in the face of adversity. Thank you for growing with me and continually growing closer to God. Together, with God in the middle, we will accomplish great things. I loved you yesterday. I love you today. I'll love you always.

To my five children, Q, K, A, C, and S, I am grateful God chose me to help aid you on your journey to greatness. I love you all very much. I love you with everything I have. May I be the mother and Mi-Mi God has called me to be for each of you. My desire is that you all have a more positive and prosperous life than I had.

To my mother, Muriel Davis, thank you for having patience with me and all my mood swings over these last few decades. You are my friend for life. No matter what happened in my life, you have been a rock that I am always able to lean on. Thank you for all the encouragement and pushing me to be the best version of myself. Thank you for everything: for your words of wisdom and for loving me unconditionally. I didn't always make it easy, but thank you. I love you for life.

To my beloved sister Zelda and to my friend Alexandra (blogger of Daisies and Cacti), without your individual contributions, *Rise* would not be where it is today. You two have been very instrumental in ensuring I published a high-quality book. You have embraced my late nights, early mornings, and last-minute requests. I love you each dearly, and I am not sure how I could repay you for your efforts. Keep rising, sisters. Zelda, you are a gem. I love you.

To my pastors, Bishop Joseph Roberts Jr. and Pastor Michelle Roberts, I am forever grateful for you wisdom, insight, late-night phone calls, and assisting me in becoming the best version of myself in Christ that I can be. I thank you for your prayers and encouragement, along with your keen prophetic eye, Bishop. You two have been a great inspiration. Jesus transformed and renewed your lives. Through you, I have learned that when He blesses you, be a blessing to others.

To my dear friend Doncella Nicholson, thank you for guiding me and holding me accountable. Accountability partners are the key to growth and development. You have heavily contributed to my development. I am grateful for you checking in and asking the hard questions. Thank you for never asking me to be someone else, but instead encouraging me to better myself every step of the way.

To my dearly departed father, Leon Davis, may he rest in peace, thank you for helping me come out of my shell and bringing the fire out of me. You saw potential in me when I did not see it in myself. You may have had some unorthodox ways of igniting my potential, but I am thankful for your persistence in requiring excellence from me. I love you forever.

To all my readers, thank you. My hope is that each page encouraged you to rise. You have also made an investment in my vision of owning a mentoring program for children. This book is my first step in that direction. Thank you, not just from me, but from the youth I will be able to help rise.

This is by no means a full list of people who have been instrumental in my development. If I could list each of you by name and deed, this book would never end. I thank my family, friends, mentors, co-workers, and everyone who has poured something into me that I was able to pour into this book. You all have helped to shape and mold me into the woman I am continually becoming.

As this book ends, it is bittersweet. I am excited and hope to encourage you all, but nervous with what is to come. The events that led to me writing this book were nothing I expected, but I accept it was necessary to grow.

There were several moments I questioned, *Why me?* Despite it all, I pushed through and remained in the present. As the trials and tribulations arose, it became increasingly more difficult, but I became confident that blessings are on the way. These events prepared me for what is to come and the role I will own in inspiring others.

I am grateful for the hardships I've endured because all of that has led me to this very moment of creating and closing *Rise*. I hope I honor every investment in my life through the way I live and the way I love my husband and children. I have been battered, bruised, tested, and frustrated, yet I've resolved to rise.

Rise.

Thank you for reading *Rise*.
I hope you've been inspired to make a difference.
If you enjoyed this book, please leave an online review.

For more inspiration
KEEP IN TOUCH WITH SHANA DANIELLE
Website: www.ShanaDanielle.com
Blog: www.ShanaDanielle.com/Its-time-to-rise-blog
Facebook: www.facebook.com/IAmShanaDanielle
Instagram: www.instagtam.com/IAmShanaDanielle
Twitter: www.twitter.com/ImShanaDanielle

www.ingramcontent.com/pod-product-compliance
Lightning Source LLC
Chambersburg PA
CBHW021110080526
44587CB00010B/455